STEEL

STEEL

poems by

ALISON PRINE

STEEL

Cider Press Review
PO BOX 33384
San Diego, CA, USA
CIDERPRESSREVIEW.COM

First edition
10 9 8 7 6 5 4 3 2 1 0

ISBN: 978-1930781207
Library of Congress Control Number: 2015957105

Cover photo,
Author photograph by Kelley Goulette
Cover design by Caron Andregg

ABOUT THE *CIDER PRESS REVIEW* BOOK AWARD:

The annual *Cider Press Review* Book Award offers a $1,500 prize, publication, and 25 author's copies of a book-length collection of poetry. For complete guidelines and information, visit CIDERPRESSREVIEW.COM/BOOKAWARD.

Printed in the United States of America
at Thomson-Shore, in Dexter, MI.

*in memory of Charles Prine, my father
and for Kel, my love*

CONTENTS

I

II

III

IV

FROM JEFFREY HARRISON, JUDGE OF THE 2014 BOOK AWARD

Two tragic events haunt this powerful first collection—the early loss of the poet's mother and her brother's death—the kind of events that "change the alignment/ of every season after" and tear open vast absences in a life.

Alison Prine bravely explores those absences here, engaging in the struggle to make something "immune to ruin" out of what is broken and to mend the connections severed by death, even while acknowledging the inability of language to fill the void left by loved ones or to find easy answers. "This isn't consolation," as she says in one poem. Instead, poem by poem, she makes a dwelling for herself and the reader, "building from the inside" while remaining attuned to the possibility of correspondences in the outside world. And through the quiet urgency of her voice, she finds "a secular way of praying." This book is a blessing.

Jeffrey Harrison

I

THE ENGINEERS TAUGHT US

to check one hundred times a day
and tomorrow we will keep on checking.

Everything is here: messages, filters, compass,
wisdom, music, news of the world,
time of day everywhere. Locators.
Something of my old life—the childhood
neighbor's laugh, burned patch
from the shag rug of 1979, phone numbers of the dead.

When I admitted that for months after his suicide
I left my brother voicemails,
my sisters all said they had called him too.
We are believers.

Dear engineers, please
put me in touch with those
who have trespassed against me.

The fortune teller will not take the engineer
to be her lawfully wedded wife.
Together they will not provide
the navigation tools to fill me
with a greenhouse of hibiscus.

My smartphone offers no shelter.
There is only building from the inside
and its necessary loneliness.
It's a terrible machine that won't
let me lose.

WHEREVER

The train I rode used to roll by here when I was on my way
out of what I have since gone back to.

I can still feel the strain of exile
as the world slipped behind,

and see, from the window, the flat water
of the lake as it replicated the sky,

purple, grey and pale yellow—
we called it "blue."

Sometimes I would step off the platform and find
the afternoon air had softened like a face asleep.

Or I would turn from the memory of losing, and there—
buttercups in the grass.

The railroad bed is now rugged with ragweed,
the old ties crumble into dirt.

Follow this rail a long, long way and you'll never get
to where I never got to either.

BROTHER AND SISTER

I notice that Wednesday keeps repeating
after a pause, like rain.

Time is the room I can't get out of.
Only in sleep can I slip through the back door.

In my dream you are alive again
a sweet reprieve where I compose a new prelude.

What you had of mine was not earned
but inscribed in the face behind my face.

A brother and sister are like magnets pulling
and repelling each other.

In our childhood games we named a "safety"
and someone to be "it."

Then we went back home again.

RINGS

My mother died young
teaching me that the soul lives
in costume jewelry
and a broken watch.

Light repeats itself with brave conviction,
a lesson in compassion
on the walls of old buildings.

Humiliation makes us better lovers,
makes us better shelters.
I learned to build by tossing stones into water.

All ghosts have the same thesis
which can be heard
deep from the throat of every morning,
sounding like an echo of your voice.

GOING BACK

Blades slap back and forth, rhythmic, decisive
but what I feel cannot be wiped clean.

Driving alone through wet snow
on a highway back to Pittsburgh

where from the sod lawns of the South Hills
through the Liberty Tunnel

there is one millisecond when descending dark
gives way to ascending dark.

You can see the circle of light ahead.
Then, suddenly, a view of sun and steel

where three rivers meet and barges
once loaded with coal float towards obscurity.

This snow goes back to the year I was born.
It came down through the steel mill's smoke

into the Ohio River, while I lay tiny in her arms
in Room 314 of Magee-Womens Hospital,

and she, exhausted, touched a finger to my cheek,
a mother's promise

she did not know she wouldn't have
the chance to keep. The sky glowed

orange at the horizon over the river
as the mills blazed on toward their finale

when they would empty into dark caves
with silences larger than the city itself.

THE TIME COMES

When it arrives I hope I am home
in an empty house with sunlight on the table.

Today is a Wednesday late in October,
probably six weeks since that black-backed gull
dragged its wing past my beach towel.
But I am bad at forgetting.

Now retroactive estrangements
clutter the calendar on my desk.

Before the time comes I'll paint my lips
like my mother did at 4:45 pm
Monday through Friday.
It was a lesson in desire after all.

I'm glad I came at the end of whatever
made them keep having children,
the sum total of their multiplication,
a tow-head, a serious girl.

There were years I managed
not to love anyone who didn't love me.
For days this summer I stared
out over the water, pretending.
The whole season tipped like a glass.

THE LITTLE LEAGUE HOURS

the town rests at the last trolley stop
ten miles to the south
of the Monongahela River
no gulls or pigeons ventured that far
only bicycle bells and white faces
bees fat and heavy in the gardens
women still smoked at kitchen tables
and I was too young to know
the homesickness of Tuesday mornings
love failed to rise up under the solar plexus
the heart's flutter replaced by a deck of cards
the lilac and crabapples
planted near young oaks and white pines
were bitter and sweet
as the casserole burned
and the Little League hours
dragged on into darkness
a woman knows when she can't feel it anymore
the phantom limb of her desire
reaching beyond the sad squares
of suburban lawns neat and safe
as a package of soap
there was a woman dreaming
who stifled a cry
I stepped on a yellow jacket
with my bare foot the summer
my mother began to shake herself loose
all these years later I can still drive by the brick house
the only thing that kept its shape
when it was over

LONG AFTER THE ACCIDENT

injuries to the face cannot be concealed
must be explained over and over
until they begin to author themselves

under the wound a hard knot forms
and takes years to loosen

sirens thread into waking and dreams
windshields shatter the steel grinding
confusion of who came through
and who didn't

by process of elimination
the ghost child is me
walking through linoleum corridors
head bandaged eyes swollen
everyone lies to her
and brings gifts

a concussion fills the mind
like a flood of cold water
the force of it erodes the soil
grasses drown

then the smoke
from a mother's last cigarette
becomes the mist
that hangs over the constant river

SURGEON

Calligraphy of bare branches
against the untainted snow.
Skin stung with cold.
February, as always, thinning
to a point, a needle that
sews shut a season of sleep.

Any more light, any sooner,
would have hurt me.
Anything more than these murmurs
in the cold, blank streets.
My hands and feet ache
in the moonlight.
My lashes hold tiny crystals
in the place where my body touches
winter, and winter recoils.

There was a man who sewed
my face after an accident
that changed the alignment
of every season after.
I wish I could thank him
for closing me so carefully,
leaving me legible
for all winters to come.

CITY OF BRIDGES

We were miles away from all three rivers,
still their convergence defined us.
Four hundred and forty-six bridges
crossing back and forth
into the grid at the city's small heart.

At the far end of the trolley line
was the good life they wanted—
for them, for us.

Back then there were just as many days
in each September.

In the lot behind the restaurant
I stood alone in a hard rain
in diluted suburban darkness
soaking my uniform through.
Torrents. Closing my eyes.
I knew that somewhere
was a gaze I wanted to walk into.

I like to be at the edge of open waters—
the feel of an amphitheater at dawn,
a rendering of *someday*.

I had a home in a city of names
I would relinquish
though the rivers always took back the rain.

DARKROOM

The earnest face of a young woman
who has just cut off her hair

appears beneath the rippling liquid
in a closet-like room lit by a single red bulb.

That year I could take only
portraits of myself.

Sometimes the self was a wooden chair,
or a frost-tipped leaf in the grass,

layers of paint peeling off bricks,
or a hinged metal lamp on a table.

Monochrome both dulled
and clarified the subject.

I was inventing an antidote—
an alternate for her hand on my forehead.

It was impossible to see that I was young
until it wasn't true any longer.

ODE TO A FORGOTTEN CONVERSATION

I sat at a diner years ago
between a man I pretended to love
and a woman I pretended not to.
I reached across to punch the buttons
on the jukebox, and poured more cream into my cup.

Music held the honesty that none of us
had yet grown into. I leaned against the strain.
We were old enough by then
to argue about the country.
Though I can't retrieve the disagreements,
I cherish all the words.

I never asked them if they felt
what I felt when I saw a gash
in a chain link fence. Or when
the tendrils of ivy grew toward each other
across the painted brick.

I wanted to stand with others
at the bus stop just to feel their kinship.
But the bus came and I didn't get on.
When the day was over
my roommate sang a cappella in the darkness;
it was the closest thing I had
to knowing someone.

CHOICE

Not having a child
is a daughter in itself—
a legacy of enoughness
or some other incapacity.

Sometimes it crawls across
your body at dawn, needing
to be calmed. Or years later
shuts a door against you.

I never planned
to take or give a name to anyone.
I needed many hours,
one against the next without
interruption,
and a stream through a forest,
water crashing over rocks
into a pool, a current,
a quickening.

I think love like that
is a bird I did not want
to fly through my window
and bruise itself against the walls.

REARVIEW MIRROR: JANUARY

My heart started beating inside you.

I think of you when the road ices over,
or when a certain scratching
brings back the old record player
that stood in the living room under the window.

Or when a road ends. When people
give explanations for why
terrible things happen.

I was there when your heart stopped beating.
I was small and sleeping
in the twisted metal and the blood.

It comes back like the sound
of those old rotary phones—
the one choking ring they make
when they're slammed against the floor.

REARVIEW MIRROR: FEBRUARY

My beginning and your ending got so close
that all traces of you in my memory
lost hold.

When I have nothing left to say,
I have you—
a series of disappearances,
a street sign, a shade of turquoise,
and a Formica table.

A few decades later
we have hundreds of sadness medications.
There is an information machine
in everyone's pocket.

We have nothing left to say,
and we keep saying it.

Take my face between your hands.
Is this what you expected?
I thought I would write this once,
and instead
it is every time.

FORTUNE TELLER

What did I want from her?
I already know
one half of life is to build,
the other half for wind to dismantle.

I know a person's gait conveys
the number of stones in their heart.
I know history is being swallowed
in the din of the television
as the screens grow larger and larger
until we will walk right into the picture.

The fortune teller promised one day
I would learn to stop breathing,
one day I could close my eyes.

Next time around I will be a city pigeon,
iridescent as a pearl. I will spread
out on the currents with my flock
and scavenge along the cement.
Please drop some crumbs for me.

THE PARTY

Blue sings a song on the porch.
Brown is the one I take for granted.
Green serves us cheese muffins and dark wine.
Green laughs and it makes us feel like laughing.
Pink sits on the steps and tells me secrets.
Purple's drunk and holds my gaze across the room.
Black loved us and we wanted to be loved.

Blue has a harmonica in his pocket.
Purple and I stand and smoke under the cottonwood.
Green won't break her promises.
Pink rustles the leaves like a cat.

Blue is the most eloquent.
Blue is with us, and at the same time,
Blue is someplace else.
Pink puts her fingers over my eyes.
Purple and I are cold in our shirtsleeves.

Blue holds the last long note.
Brown never asks for more.
Green stacks the plates by the sink.
Green throws her head back, laughing.
Pink taps at the glass like mist.
Purple couldn't say what purple meant.
Black loved us and we wanted to be loved.

IF, THEN

If you are the answer,
then it is a question of meteorology.

If the wind is from the north,
then your grandmother fled her country
to find her way back.

If we are to return to our purpose,
then we first have to leave the impressions
of our mouths on our promises.

If taking your face between my palms is a promise,
then I will sleep like a sky full of geese.

If migration is based on an internal compass,
then I will go back to taking pictures of myself.

If a self-portrait is a historical document,
then this is a story of shoulders and elbows
against a window of snow.

I AM SORRY

For the moments in which
I did not recognize you.

That your love for me was like August—
lush and fast and full of thicket

while I loved you like December—
dark and spare and everlasting.

I walked into your church
wanting something outside the doctrine.

Sorry the things I got close to believing
were caught up in your yellow hair

and the freckles splashed across your chest.
I am sorry that I have

no second language with which
I could grow to understand my first.

What have you broken open
and turned away from in all these years?

I can't recall your laugh
but I remember waking each morning

with your long limbs wound around me
and wanting to throw them off.

LAKESHORE

Light carves through the water
as it sucks at the rocks.

Behind us a choke of woods
stands bloomless and overgrown.

You start to tell me
you are going back to Asheville,

as though you could dismantle
everything our hands have done.

Erase the scent of sun-warmed pine,
black willow, oak.

Undo our kiss,
bruised with regret.

I know that you've unlatched me,
and would again.

But, in the gentleness of this air
every thing holds its grace:

the duck's orange foot
waving beneath the algae,

swallows arching
over the thin horizon,

my certain gesture
of turning

toward you,
before turning away.

WHAT HAPPENED

Every arc on this shore
tells our story—
a wind-raveled tree line
smear of red in the mid-day sky.

I am captivated by incrementally smaller things.
Once it was the dying back of oceans
war in countries I'd never been to
later the women in my town
then those who could love me
then you,

your face, the tip of your finger
the eyelash that just slipped down your cheek.

To watch it gives a sense of floating:
July and the body of the lake is loose and warm
and gestures toward me
even as it crawls invisibly back into the sky.

Our story is like that small child
screaming wildness as she chases the herring gull along the sand—
what if she could catch that bird,
what then?

Is that what happened to us?

CEREMONY

crows in the butternut announce
that morning is on speaking terms
with the night

what will become of last night's words
said to you in anger

will we lift them in our arms
and fold them
ever so carefully, methodically
like the janitors who take down
the flag in the evenings
    it goes like this
    and then like this
making a tight triangle

will we let them dissolve in the soft confusion
of light on leaves

or will they go their common distance
then come to rest
with all the other snow geese in the field

INFIDELITY

The tide withdraws in silence.
The whole landscape shifts as you sleep
in the house behind me—
or lie in the white sheets
thinking about your new desires.

Flocks of grackles come west
along the harbor, skimming the roof tops.
I hear their wings as they push the air.

A muscle in me quivers against the remnant
of last night's dream—
the simple wooden boat, jewelweed
jangling from its thin stalk,
my own hand, restless, tentative,
darkened with sun.

The answer is simple—
I want to touch you, despite everything,
whoever you are.

JANUARY 1ST

the year is new but I am lost
how will I learn to lie down without you?
I am bitter with exhaustion
the sky heavy as a bag of salt

how will I learn to lie down without you?
as I stand on the end of the fishing pier
the sky heavy as a bag of salt
the snow came suddenly, but comes down slowly

as I stand on the end of the fishing pier
gazing into the big lonesome body of the lake
the snow came suddenly, but comes down slowly
I watch the white dots disappear

into the big lonesome body of the lake
black as a day window
I watch the white dots disappear
into the gray slick surface without a trace

black as a day window
the lake swallows the town's series of mistakes
into the gray slick surface without a trace
breathing ever so slightly

the lake swallows the town's series of mistakes
this is how the moments pass
breathing ever so slightly
coming down onto me and disappearing into me

this is how the moments pass
I am bitter with exhaustion
coming down onto me and disappearing into me
the year is new but I am lost

JANUARY THAW

Unseasonable rain
forces itself into our conversations.

We can't help but acknowledge
that winter has fallen apart.

You and I still here
in the story of the other.

When night rolls over us
there is a feeling of being spared.

I count on January to come back to itself
toughening up the weeping fields.

Still, we lean toward a transformation, if not
in this life, then in the one this life conjures up.

WHAT IT TAKES

Is there an apology here?
The seventeen necessary parts,
including one full downpour
on an October afternoon
and bright red leaves
wet on the pavement.

A particular laugh
cut with sorrow
and a mirror cracked by a fist
near the doorway.

Regret wears furrows
into the floorboards. It takes
a gull's view—all those distances—
looking down at the mouths
of rivers from the sky.

And of course the love of language—
how it bears our clumsy burden
like a backhoe in the morning light
lifting its great forehead from the dirt.

NAMING THE WAVES

Above the harbor these clouds refuse to be described
except in the language with which they describe themselves.
I stand here in the morning stillness.

Which is of course not a stillness,
the sky spreading open in the east with amber light
while drifting away to the west.

Here I can sense how the world
spins us precisely in its undetectable turn
somehow both towards and away.

The blue of the harbor holds
the sky in its calm gaze.
This is a love poem, be patient.

Between you and me nothing leaves,
everything gathers.
I will name for you each wave rolling up on the harbor sand:

> *this is the first breath of sleep*
> *this the cloth of your mother's dress*
> *this the cadence of our long conversation*

I want to show you how everything
on this harbor has been broken:
shells, glass, rust, bones and rock—

Crushed into this expanse of glittering sand,
immune to ruin, now rocking
in the slow exhale of the tide.

RESEMBLANCE

The poinsettia bleeds milk
from the broken leaf. Those are not blossoms.

Snow fills in and covers up.

You are reading a book
about sisters talking.
I write down everything
we won't say.

What we shared:
the meals—hundreds, thousands even:
flank steak, shit-on-a-shingle, fish sticks—
long before *your* house and pesto
and you're a mother and I'm not

and the snow comes back.

*

People say we look alike
But we spent years
not being alike,
through all the sting
and scrape of childhood,
through all the smallness,
all the nearness, the questions.

At this point there are no surprises.
Each comfort, each hurt falls
where the groove is worn.

I was four and you were seven
and the snow caused it.

*

Our story is so long it outlasts us.
I am going to bed on an air mattress
on your daughter's bedroom floor.
It is Christmas Eve.
Forty years ago we slept on bunk beds
in the brick house on Folkstone Drive
while our parents argued in whispers
on what would be their last night together.

The snow had already begun.

*

I would throw myself in front of a train
for you. Isn't that the expression?

But our story doesn't go like that.
We were in the back seat,
and no one could stop
the car skidding over the dotted line.

It was Christmas
so it will always be
balsam and sugar and milk from a stem.

*

I hate it in the movies when
they kill off the woman

to make us love her.
But it worked for our mother

didn't it?

*

When I go by the sliding glass
of an emergency room entrance
and I glimpse the faces
of two people leaning
anxiously towards one another
on the stiff plastic chairs

I think, *that's you*
that's me.

THE YEAR AFTER HIS SUICIDE

We have gone through
so many revisions of the prelude
that we no longer know
who stood together in the storm.

I like the first and seventh versions:
the sun broke through the trees and the moist
furtive air moved around us
and in us and from us and
carried us
into these exact distances,
these confusions and omissions.

The things we wish we'd said
turn to milkweed seeds.
In them the property of flight conflicts
with the idea of taking root.

I bequeath all the grey and tender mornings
of where we are now
to what occasionally wakes us.

When I strain for a final conveyance
all I hear is the cold applause
of October rain over asphalt.
Since that river ran through our hands
even the endings
don't have endings.

BROTHER

Each of us with the same
lipsticked ghost, sitting in her
turquoise dress, head in hand.

Is she crying? Has she said
our names?

For the sixth time in twenty years
we spoke and you said,
"Turkeys come to this field
at the end of summer,
light comes through the trees
like a stage spot for a monologue
I've been writing all my life.
I'd perform it for you now—
but isn't the sky too heavy
with salt?"

MOTHER

Would you appear in this blue kitchen
a flour smear on your forehead?
I'm creaming the butter with my knuckles.
I'm cooking in the dark.

Would you recognize me
now that the snow geese have tucked
their heads beneath their wings?
Now that the wind has shaken loose my back door?

Would you step close to me,
trace your index finger along my cheek?
The air tonight is full.
It's two a.m., and a red light shines

through the cottonwood silks
as they drift toward the street.
I can hear the floor boards creaking
as you shift your weight.

THE LAST DAY

This is what they mean
by time running out.

What they mean by variegated
when grief comes at the onset of flowers.

This is what we're left to
as if violets weren't already
painful and plentiful and brief.

I say "we" but what I mean
is time, I mean the sky at 7:30 PM
or even now, the sky,
however you pronounce it—
isn't the same here as it was then,
with him, as it was
arching over him, allowing him.

This is what they mean
by the last time.

If the world is round
then so is the sky
which will come back repeating
the lilacs and dandelions
no matter what we do.

This is what they mean by grafting,
when you try to make one thing
into something else.

STEEL

he kept it in the box, unopened
through the yearning and the darkness, driving on alone

all the nourishment he found
in silver cans and cellophane wrappers

till exhaustion brought him dreams
of falling and flying and strange fields

through the windshield he saw
the dumb sadness of animals and the grace of long grasses

sometimes he heard someone's voice
(though he was alone) and took comfort

he watched the telephone wires and kinglets
and dirty little sparrows

he wished for rain, or the desire for rain
or the memories which rain evokes

when he took it out, the gun felt
like he thought it would, clean and smooth

as water running through his hands
the cold pull of a river rising

THE FIRST GREY MORNINGS

Grim hours work at the patina.
A harsh rain courses.
Detail by detail it changes the surfaces
as the sky grows frantic.

A harsh rain courses;
the wind courses. The family,
as the sky grows frantic,
continues roughly on its course.

The wind courses, the family
together for days after in a Route 19 hotel
continues roughly on its course
lost in the thick of want

together for days after in a Route 19 hotel.
None of us can go to sleep,
lost in the thick of want
just to see again the light hay color of his eyes.

None of us can go to sleep.
Our unopened letters on the seat of his pickup.
Just to see again the light hay color of his eyes.
We calculate our helplessness, our fault.

Our unopened letters on the seat of his pickup—
it seems we've lost our hold.
We calculate our helplessness, our fault,
and we have the answer.

It seems we've lost our hold.
We want an answer,
but, we have the answer,
we just don't have the question.

We want an answer
or the correct alignment of stars.
We just don't have the question
or the time the question needs

or the correct alignment of stars
and conjunctions which would make
the time the question needs
work as a hand grasping.

Conjunctions which would make
asking the question to our brother
work as a hand grasping.
We want to go back

asking the question to our brother,
hear the large gravelly timbre of his voice.
We want to go back
to a long conversation sitting in his truck.

Hear the large gravelly timbre of his voice:
detail by detail it changes the surfaces,
a long conversation sitting in his truck.
Grim hours work at the patina.

STRANGER

A glazed field can hold strong in deep cold
but the midday sun thaws it into tatters.

The kid with the tattooed face
asks for my spare change.
This is my offering—

I forced myself to look at his face,
unflinching.

I stood next to the husk of him
laid out in a stranger's shirt and tie
and touched his honey brown hair.

Now all strangers feel
a little like my brother.

The police report said
he was homeless—
but he had a home.
We cleaned it bare in three days,
the five of us.

Since then, all things are,
at times, strange. Comb, spoon,
ceiling—and the hammering
inside.

A half-unwrapped cough drop
sits on the side table.

Each painting too much like
a mouth that isn't moving.

When I lie awake
he is the hawk, hovering over,
as if my sleep
were his meadow.

TO BIDE

water over stones over water
  blue of an uncomplicated sky
    the merciful indifference of that hue

and in the great curve
  of morning clearness, one star—
    my dead star—

pierces and shines
    and shines

I WOULD LIKE TO SPEAK
TO THE MAN IN CHARGE

The racket is like a drawer of silver
clattering to the floor.

This morning outside my kitchen window
a sharp-shinned hawk
tore apart a yellow bird
in the apple tree.

What do you propose we do when our questions
become useless?

Every day, I forgive you these messes.

Goodness is not a false positive. The bloodline
is not a false positive—nor are the ghosts
who raised me.

Go ahead and wield your mighty blankness,
I too can sing into my pillow,
sir.

VIGIL

Be careful of souvenirs,
they cannot conceal
the ache of a yellow room.

Be careful of arrivals,
they will disperse like the wet
dark wool of a morning sky.

When I was a girl
I picked crabapples out of the grass.
Now what am I gathering?

This year, too, is getting lost
among our belongings.
Outside the trees let loose.

Their regretted leaves
now brittle and bright
skitter across the pavement.

ORCHARD

Hundreds of miles south of here
my father tends a windowsill of African violets.

In the summer of 1999 my brother harvested
black cherries in Virginia.

The sun was like a smile
that cut both ways.

I wish I knew how many trees
it takes to make a reason.

At that latitude you can't find
enough nicotine comfort to fill a bucket.

Though there's a view of the Blue Ridge Mountains
that looks like everything will turn out.

When an old man pinches yellow leaves from the soil,
velvet petals brush against his fingers.

This isn't consolation.
It's another season in a man's life.

FORGETTING

Eyes sting with pollen in the new green of April
        while grey clouds sag like a worn pillow.

I want to forget
        the sound of 10,000 white geese rising
            over a fallow corn field stiff with frost.

I want to forget you.

A weeping cherry hides in her chest
        a nest of hornets that drift out one by one
          over the water.

A mother's voice like a warm hand across your forehead
        though she was gone
            riding horses far into the past while you

spent a thousand hours in an old rural theater
        deciding how light would cross the landscape
          and the space beneath the line.

It can last forever, the moment of beauty:
        the roar of snow geese like a fevered ovation
         rippling in the sky.

INTO APPLES

I intend to outlive the sad girl from Pennsylvania.
I intend to get as close to indivisible
as a girl from Pennsylvania can.
Yes, and turn the burial ground we never visited
into its very own September.
In this there will be a transformation—
a love affair of sunlight and grass
gently, deliberately, turning
sadness into apples.

IV

DISPLACE

I haven't lived there for thirty-one years
but my unicorn decal shines in the bedroom window.

Through the floor we felt the deep vibration of the central air unit
that hunkered beside the house.

Hollow doors, drywall, thick patterned drapes,
scratches on the records, and the sheen of new linoleum.

Before me now—a rowboat named Patience, and a ruby drink
on the railing against the fog at dusk.

Here the cicadas in the nearby beech forest sing
up into the bare curves of the sand dunes.

A red fox slips through the marsh grasses
as the tide pulls the sea slowly off the breakwater.

I am teaching myself to identify birds
by the sound of their wings.

I am transposing this landscape
with the one I was born into.

A secular way of praying:
flock of cormorants gliding through the mist.

ON THE HARBOR

The gulls call harsher and harsher
then fall silent.
The plovers and sanderlings call
teacup, bluette,
please, please, please

Far out on the harbor
an old fishing boat rattles awake.
I hear in it my father's voice
turning in me such tenderness
I break
like a thin purple oyster shell, pieces so small
teacup, bluette,
please, please

Pleasing blue, old boats
weathering and tipping in the low tide,
reminding me that we, too, run aground
from every water
from everyone we father.

He would want to know what gull, exactly,
keeping a list.
Firsts are very important.

I am the last of his children.
I will spend the least of his life with him.
I will say, *ringbilled, Dad, immature,*
I will say

Summer is ending again.
And that is what my father says to me.

WATERMARK

This morning I notice congregations.
Moorings, sanderlings, even rubbish seems
to have a being together, an affiliation through proximity.
A jet tears through the clouds
giving the sunrise a beautiful scar.
Every landscape is autobiographical.
I recognize my own industrious rhythms in a gathering
of blackbirds on the sand. Boat and bird noises
like kitchen music from childhood, efficient
clipped movements of a woman who raised me
but has long been gone.
The difference between the ocean
and a picture of the ocean:
distracting inflatables, a fog horn, car engines,
the piercing cry of an old herring gull,
burn of salt in the eye or sting of sand fleas,
ropes clanging against masts,
a dog barking insistently in the distance
on and on without pause, maybe in distress or pleading
or announcing something of great importance
over the harbor, over the sand and out to the sea.

GRAND ISLE FERRY CROSSING

Come out in rain.

The geese are filling the sky.

I had a grandmother I never dream about.
I never even went upstairs in her house.

There are ways to find out the things no one will tell you.
I eavesdropped through childhood.
I rummaged through my parents' dresser drawers.

Yet, the greatest mysteries still hovered beyond my reach,
above the pink cushioned layers of insulation.
I never knew,
I still don't know.

Shoes and a box of buttons,
I walked from room to room.

As my grandmother died, I watched my father.
He paced the linoleum floor, stopping
to sift through papers by the phone.

When I stand on the deck of this ferry,
I am a movie star, wearing a trench coat.
The first scene is a tragic one,
where the young girl's mother dies.

The girl grows up, and her face remains soft.

The trick is to strike an interesting pose,
head turned, face to the wind,
both elbows leaning on the rail.

I am growing my hair for the part.

TAKING STOCK

Out with the actualized—
but keep the howl of my foxhound mutt
from my backyard in the 1980's.
He was a reliable source of comfort.
Even when I dreamed of nuclear annihilation,
even when I tried to push the years
faster forward and failed.

Out with agile limbs, full lips
all those early, unearned gifts.
I must make room for what time is doing to my face.
And for these nights that drop deeper from
the daylight, and dreams that tear
like cirrus clouds in the flare
of my alarm clock.

Out with the chicken heart,
the rush and stumble.
Out with the pretty comforts.
In with the low groan of the sump-pump
its birth song from the basement—
spring coming at me like a fist.

Out with each failed tenderness,
there is no second chance. Out with every town
I drove through but never tried to belong in.
Out with all the yellow photographs, even they
have lost the past. And words, worse than silence.

NEAR

sort of half eavesdropping on two sisters having
egg sandwiches and coffee at the next table
I look out through fogged windows at the flurries
bewildered by northern and westerly winds
the blonde sister asks the other one how
she navigated her now defunct love affair with Jason
who was 'not political' then a garbage truck rumbles
down the alley creating a nostalgic veil of noise
that wraps me back into New Year's Day
about a week ago when I walked alone on Texaco Beach
and a great blue heron flew close overhead in slow ballet
the year already seemed clouded with loneliness
and I can't help thinking about the quote scribbled
in the stall in the 1st floor bathroom
of Jefferson Junior High School
love: may your being become ever clearer to me
even those many years ago I remember feeling a sense
of humanity's blue ruin and how we are
concealed behind words and gestures
later on my New Year's walk the woods
filled with crows calling the darkness home
and in the near dusk the snow hung prettily
in the pine boughs by the ice sculpted cliffs
and the crows seemed to be saying that snow
isn't meant to cushion us and that they
are the gathering ones and we are the dispersing ones
and the clouds slid down to the horizon
like a nearly closed eye and the sun burned
a cool 40 watt light over the water
I know that the redbud in the back yard
doesn't have a chance it already leans sideways
under the towering butternut that devours the light

showing how little it matters to be beautiful
it's just the mischance of what grows up near us
now the sisters have fallen into a silence
I could call 'comfortable' but I know better

THOUGHTS IN RIJKSMUSEUM

through the purified air
there are many languages
and through the languages
conflicting ideas
about nearness

it's orange vellum
it's a fat black line
it's the eyes of the
security guard standing
specifically in that corner
for these hours she
like the artist
is coming back from madness
I recognize it in the lines
of her mouth
like the lines in the painting
they are my lines

she seems to be drawing nearer
orange touches blue
and the angle is a convergence
that could last all our lives:
a spiral, an orchard, an apple tree in bloom,
a scattering of strangers on a beach,
a block of blue, silver grid,
a uniform

what can you ask
in this intentional space?
we all move slowly, deliberately
as if blocking a play

as if we are rehearsing
and she has the part of a security guard
and I a woman who might
become her lover if only
I spoke Dutch and Italian
and German and French
if only I knew the color of fragility
the kind that transforms the clean
white rooms and corridors
into nearness

there are so many pieces
so many rooms
so many questions
that I have to leave her
I sit on a bench in the hallway
someone speaks kindly to me
in a language I can't understand
I can see that this is not happiness
but so little is happiness

CROSSING

Sherry Lewis had a pink television in her bedroom.
Her newly pierced ears oozed bloody puss.
We were five years old.
She had a boxer named Tiny,
a poodle named Sugar,
and my mother was dead.

I couldn't sleep at Sherry Lewis' house.
I walked the carpeted hallways
while her parents, her brother, Sherry
lay still and the dogs twitched in the darkness.
I wanted to slip out and cross the street
to my house but I couldn't, I knew it already—
it is impossible to get back,
though you can see it from the slit in the curtain.

THE GIRL IN THE RED SHOES

finds the dead pigeon
and cries, but still loves
the marmalade cat, so when
she sees her mother
lie down with the white-haired
neighbor, she has had some practice
in dismantling the landscape.

The girl in the red shoes
walks down to the railroad tracks
that go along the riverbank
and in the riverbank the girl
pokes something with a stick.
She is choosing between explanations.
The girl in the red shoes
finds a whole blue egg
in the dirt.

AT THE END OF THE STORY

They found her asleep in their child's bed.
Looking like a child herself, a thin line of spit
glistening from the corner of her mouth.
She was beautiful, so those who described her
said *touched* or *lost* instead of *crazy*.
There was her thick tangle of yellow curls,
and a bright greenness in her eyes.
She had been there a while.
She had run her small hands among their things,
eaten from the dishes, moved from chair to chair
looking for the one she could rest in.
She dozed in their child's bed,
dirt-caked shoes kicked to the floor.
There are so many kinds of tiredness:
hers had a magnetic force
and a metallic taste at the back of the throat.
Outside a flock of starlings
moved as one into the hemlock.
Fall had just leaned into the forest.
She dreamed the same dream
spitting her broken teeth into her hand.
It didn't matter how perfect the bed was,
the dreams came with her,
even into a stranger's house on an autumn afternoon.
She sensed before she woke
the fierceness of their protection
and the warm, heavy softness of how they loved.

JULY

The only music the slow slap of harbor waves
mixing with the bird sounds
that I would hear if it were August—
I know their calls
more clearly in their absence.

Mid-summer roses climb wild
up into the scrub oaks
and across the fences, blooming thickly
in the heat. The kind of fullness
between the in breath and the out breath
while the foghorn keeps count.

The migrating birds are still far
on other shores. I want to love
everyone right now as much
as I will love them when they're gone.

FORECAST

There are good numbers and bad numbers.
Especially now, awaiting the results.
I wish we were together on a walk along the water,
pausing to stare shoulder to shoulder
over the golden grasses of the Ossabaw marsh.

It seems that the weather advises us
carefully — language of pressure and moisture
explains more accurately what lies ahead
than the white coated prophets we rely on.

This morning I woke long before dawn
and asked the sky to foretell the eventuality
with as slow a spinning away as possible.

The answer was a cliche, ambiguous
and heavy and wet. I can't remember
if we want the numbers to go higher or lower—
or to simply dissolve and reabsorb
into a mixed precipitation that will,
like a notion, tap against us from inside.

RETROSPECT

Wary of more words, more arrangements,
too many already
and the labor of their use.

Sometimes there is only one word
for everything you need.

Syllables strain like someone learning the violin
or a needle skipping in the groove
until lifted in the curl of a careful finger.

My brother's orphaned pickup idling in the background,
a word for dying of sadness.

He left a paper cup of violets on the dashboard,
which follow me to every page.

SONG ON THE WATERFRONT

I was here before the shed came down.
I photographed the weeds
against the boarded-up door.
I walked here with my camera,
my chest full of nails and salt.

I came along the railroad tracks
overgrown with loosestrife and ragweed.
I passed a woman singing in a cement field
believing she was alone.

I was here before the shed came down.
I took my picture on the rusted iron ramp.
I wanted it to look like I was walking
off the tip of the world and someone
behind me had just called my name.

ACKNOWLEDGEMENTS

Deep thanks to my poet friends who have supported me in the making of this book: Ben Aleshire, Eve Alexandra, Sue Burton, Jari Chevalier, Penelope Cray, Rachel Daley, Karin Gottshall, Marylen Grigas, Major Jackson, Kerrin McCadden, Alison Moncrief Bromage, Emily Skoler, Emilie Stigliani and Joan White.

I am grateful to the following journals in which these poems first appeared:

Chautauqua Literary Journal	"Song on the Waterfront"
Faultline	"January Thaw"
The Fourth River	"Grande Isle Ferry Crossing"
Green Mountains Review	"Brother and Sister," "The Time Comes," "Surgeon," "The Last Day," "Into Apples,"
GMR Online	"Fortune Teller"
Greensboro Review	"Rearview Mirror: January"
Harvard Review	"Naming the Waves"
The Louisville Review	"If, Then"
Michigan Quarterly Review	"The engineers taught us"
The Midwest Quarterly	"On the Harbor," "Stranger"
The Pinch	"Orchard," "Wherever"
Pittsburgh Post-Gazette	"Going Back," "City of Bridges"
Poet Lore	"Resemblance"
Poetry Letter & Literary Review	"The Girl in the Red Shoes"
Prairie Schooner	"I would like to speak to the man in charge"
The Salon	"Taking Stock"
Shenandoah	"Ode to a Forgotten Conversation," "Displace"
The South Carolina Review	"January 1st," "Steel"
The Sow's Ear Poetry Review	"The Party"
Tar River Poetry	"Lakeshore"
The Virginia Quarterly Review	"The Year After His Suicide"
WomenArts Quarterly	"Choice"